ROCK LYRICS
TRIVIA QUIZ

"featuring pop/rc

from the 1950s & 1

--(pre-British Invasion)--

400 ROCK LYRICS QUESTIONS
VOLUME 1

*an encyclopedia of rock & roll's

most memorable lyrics

in question/answer format*

by: Presley Love

Published by Hi-Lite Publishing Co.

Copyright © 2018 by:
Raymond Karelitz
Hi-Lite Publishing Company
Rock-&-Roll Test Prep Hawaii
P.O. Box 6071
Kaneohe, Hawaii 96744

email comments/corrections: rocktrivia@test-prepHi.com
(808) 261-6666

2018 (updated from 1992 edition)

Love, Presley

ROCK LYRICS TRIVIA QUIZ BOOK (1955-1964)
Volume 1 (128 pages)

1. Rock-&-Roll Quiz Book   I. Love, Presley   II. Title: Rock and Roll

2. Music

COVER DESIGN: Doug Behrens

ISBN: 978-1563910043

Printed In The United States of America

----

text collection by: **Presley Love**
format/production by: Raymond Karelitz

A Magical Musical Tour Through the Past

Once you open this book, you will be transported back to the time of magical musical memories, a mosaic of music at your fingertips!

Browse through the streets where the '50s & '60s still rule. Test your rock-trivia expertise — invite your friends to see who's the ROCK LYRICS KING!

Rock & Roll is here to stay, and now every memory-making word can be recalled whenever you feel like escaping to the past, groovin' where no person has gone before! Put on your oldies records, let their words of wisdom come alive for you, then sit back in ecstasy and let the good vibrations take you on a magic swirling ship headed on a collision course with the classics!

****

To be best prepared for this book, listen to lots of rock & roll — heavily energized with the King, Chuck Berry, R&B and Buddy Holly — and be sure not to forget the Shirelles, Crystals and Chubby Checker. For added flavor, locate the nearest jukebox at your favorite malt shop for even more Rock & Roll!

[caution: a limbo-stick can cause uncontrollable happiness, Daddio!]

The Legacy of Presley Love

In 1992, music-aficionado Presley Love compiled a vast treasure of rock & roll lyric-memoribilia, including songs from the earliest days of rock & roll up through the late '80s. This musical quiz-format collection lay dormant except for the release of a single volume which contained 400 questions. The original book — printed in 1992 — became, over the years, an Amazon.com favorite, with very positive response from those who loved the book for its "party-flavor" appeal.

In 2014, the entire vault of Presley Love's music-lyric memoribilia was located in a storage locker — containing his collection of lyric-questions and trivia questions in quiz format! It has taken 4 years of diligent compiling and organizing to create what amounts to the entire Presley Love collection of rock lyrics, rock titles and rock trivia books in quiz-format!

We are proud to unveil *ROCK LYRICS QUIZ BOOK* (1955-1964), a special 3-volume series of memorable classics. We sincerely hope you enjoy these fabulous rock-favorites in quiz-format from Presley Love's truly incredible treasure trove of rock & roll memories 1955-1989 collection!

If you're brave enough to test your skills,
here's a simple SCORING CHART:

(questions are worth 1 point each — "Harder Questions" are worth 2 points each . . . If you are able to correctly answer the question without the three choices, you receive twice the point value!)

If you score . . .

20+ Points: You probably STILL think it's 1957!
(Check your wardrobe!)

16–19: You probably paid more attention to
rock & roll than books & school!
(Check your report card!)

11–15: There's a lot of rock & roll memories
in your blood!

6–10: Don't you wish you'd listened more closely
to rock & roll ?!
(It's never too late to be hip!)

0–5: Where were YOU when rock began to rule ?!
*(Time to get experienced —
run to your music store now!!!)*

ROCK LYRICS QUESTIONS

Quiz 1

1. At what hour are Bill Haley & His Comets going to have some fun in *Rock Around the Clock*?

     a. 1:00am

     b. midnight

     c. 10:00pm

****

2. According to Frank Sinatra, what do *Love and Marriage* go together like?

     a. a bed and breakfast

     b. a horse and carriage

     c. bag and baggage

****

3. In *I Want You to Be My Girl*, what don't Frankie Lymon & the Teenagers want you to do?

     a. put their love on ice

     b. treat them badly

     c. cheat on them

****

4. What is it that you've left the Platters to do all alone in *The Great Pretender*?

     a. start a new life

     b. fall in love

     c. dream

5. What do the Chordettes want *Mr. Sandman* to bring them?

        a. a good night's sleep

        b. happiness

        c. a dream

****

6. When Chuck Berry says to *Roll Over, Beethoven,* who does he say to tell the news to?

        a. to you

        b. to Rover

        c. to Tchaikovsky

****

7. In *Tonight You'll Belong to Me,* what do Patience & Prudence also know?

    a. that you belong to somebody new

    b. that they're gonna love you forever

    c. that you'll be on your way when the morning comes

****

8. What has happened to Ivory Joe Hunter *Since I Met You Baby*?

    a. his whole life has changed

    b. he's lost his job and all his friends

    c. he's been walking on a cloud of love

9. According to the Five Satins' *In The Still of the Night,* in which month do they remember the night's stars shining brightly above?

        a. May

        b. June

        c. every month

****

10. In *Don't Be Angry,* what do the Crew-Cuts want you to let them do?

        a. stay

        b. hold your hand

        c. kiss you goodnight

****

11. According to the Four Aces, who is singing the *Melody of Love*?

        a. the eagle and the turtle dove

        b. those who never get enough

        c. a choir of angels from above

****

12. Though it may make Him sad to see the way we live, what does Al Hibbler say *He* will always do?

        a. give us another chance

        b. give us peace of mind

        c. forgive

13. How fast does Chuck Berry say *Maybellene* was driving when he caught up with her?

      a. 120 m.p.h.

      b. 95 m.p.h.

      c. faster than the speed of light

****

14. To what question do the Four Lads reply *No, Not Much*?

  a. whether they like to be with you

  b. whether they like your parents

  c. whether they'd like it if you were to go away

****

15. In *I Want You, I Need You, I Love You*, what is it that Elvis Presley thought he could live without until he met you?

      a. beer

      b. romance

      c. girls

****

16. In *Just Walking In the Rain,* why is Johnnie Ray so alone and blue?

a. because his heart still remembers you

b. because he loves you, but you haven't a clue

c. because you told him that their romance is through

HARDER QUESTIONS (17-20): 2 points each
(4 points if you can answer the question without the three choices !)

17. In *Friendly Persuasion,* what does Pat Boone want you to put on?
- **a.** your jacket and blue jeans
- **b.** your bonnet, cape and glove
- **c.** his favorite blue blouse with your lavendar dress

****

18. What does Nat 'King' Cole say may happen if you *Smile* ?
- **a.** the whole world will smile with you
- **b.** the sun will come shining through for you
- **c.** you'll see life in a different way

****

19. What do the Robins say they'll never do at *Smokey Joe's Cafe* ?
- **a.** order chili beans and rice
- **b.** smoke a cigarette
- **c.** eat there again

****

20. When the Danderliers asked their baby what she means when she says *Chop Chop Boom,* what did she say that it reminded her of ?
- **a.** a dance
- **b.** a busted head
- **c.** her mother-in-law

Quiz 1

1. **a.** 1:00am
2. **b.** a horse and carriage
3. **a.** put their love on ice
4. **c.** dream
5. **c.** a dream
6. **c.** to Tchaikovsky
7. **a.** that you belong to somebody new
8. **a.** his whole life has changed
9. **a.** May
10. **a.** stay
11. **c.** a choir of angels from above
12. **c.** forgive
13. **b.** 95 m.p.h.
14. **c.** whether they'd like it if you were to go away
15. **b.** romance
16. **a.** because his heart still remembers you

****

Questions 17-20: **HARDER QUESTIONS**

17. **b.** your bonnet, cape and glove
18. **b.** the sun will come shining through for you
19. **c.** eat there again
20. **b.** a busted head

Quiz 2

1. In *Rock & Roll Music,* under what condition does Chuck Berry not like jazz music?
   - a. if they try to change the melody
   - b. when the words aren't clear
   - c. if he isn't performing it

****

2. When did Little Richard find that his *Lucille* was not around?
   - a. last night
   - b. just now
   - c. this morning

****

3. On what Hawaiian isle did Buddy Knox find his *Hula Love* ?
   - a. the Isle of Man
   - b. the Isle of Manulani
   - c. the Isle of Phila-Lilla

****

4. In *I'm Walkin'*, what is Fats Domino hoping ?
   - a. that he'll get a ride
   - b. that he'll make it home again
   - c. that you'll come back to him

5. In *Great Balls of Fire*, what does Jerry Lee Lewis do that shows how nervous he is?
  a. he bites his lip
  b. he twiddles his thumbs
  c. he swallows his tongue

****

6. Though *You're a Thousand Miles Away*, what do the Heartbeats still have to remember you by?
  a. your love
  b. your letters
  c. memories

****

7. When Elvis Presley says *Treat Me Nice*, he expects you to scratch his back and
_____.
  a. make him purr
  b. rub his tummy
  c. run your fingers through his hair

****

8. In *I'm Sorry*, what do the Platters say that they should have known from the start?
  a. that they'd fall for you hard
  b. that they'd break your heart
  c. that you and they would someday part

9. In *You Are My Destiny,* what does Paul Anka say is the only thing that can take your love from him?

   a. your love for another man
   b. the end of the world
   c. heaven

****

10. How old is Bobby Darin's *Queen of the Hop* ?

   a. thirteen
   b. sixteen
   c. nineteen

****

11. In worrying about their *Problems,* what do the Everly Brothers wonder?

   a. whether they'll get worse with each passing day
   b. whether they'll work out right or wrong
   c. whether there's a cure for them

****

12. According to the McGuire Sisters, when is *Sugartime* ?

   a. anytime that you're near
   b. whenever they're hungry
   c. whenever you flash your sweet sweet smile

13. What do the Crew-Cuts say that you should tell the *Angels in the Sky*?

    a. all the things you've been dreaming of

    b. how much you're really in love

    c. that you're lonely

****

14. In *Why Don't They Understand,* what does George Hamilton IV say that others say about him and you?

    a. that love can't be yours today

    b. that his love for you will soon fade away

    c. that you and he will soon find out
       that love is a hurtin' thing

****

15. What does Pat Boone say can happen to *April Love*?

    a. it can slip through your fingers

    b. it can change your whole life through

    c. it can make your dreams come true

****

16. Because he wants you to *Love Me,* how would Elvis Presley feel if you were to go away?

    a. free to love another

    b. lonely

    c. more in love with you

17. What is it that the Harptones want you to *Gimme Some* of ?

        a. your sweet sweet kisses

        b. your happiness

        c. your money

****

18. In *The Church Bells May Ring,* what do the Diamonds call you?

        a. an angel in spring

        b. the song in their heart

        c. the queen of their throne

****

19. In *Just Because,* if you would expect Lloyd Price to sit and cry if you left, what does he say he'd rather do?

        a. let you go

        b. get you back

        c. smile and let it be

****

20. Where did Larry Williams finally marry *Short Fat Fannie* ?

        a. on the dock of the bay

        b. on Blueberry Hill

        c. on the dance floor

1. **a.** if they try to change the melody
2. **c.** this morning
3. **c.** the Isle of Phila-Lilla
4. **c.** that you'll come back to him
5. **b.** he twiddles his thumbs
6. **a.** your love
7. **c.** run your fingers through his hair
8. **b.** that they'd break your heart
9. **c.** heaven
10. **b.** sixteen
11. **b.** whether they'll work out right or wrong
12. **a.** anytime that you're near
13. **c.** that you're lonely
14. **a.** that love can't be yours today
15. **a.** it can slip through your fingers
16. **b.** lonely

****

Questions 17-20: HARDER QUESTIONS

17. **a.** your sweet sweet kisses
18. **c.** the queen of their throne
19. **a.** let you go
20. **b.** on Blueberry Hill

Quiz 3

1. In *Ain't Got No Home,* what does Clarence "Frogman" Henry say he sings like?

        a. Caruso

        b. a bird

        c. a frog

****

2. In *Shake, Rattle and Roll,* what do Bill Haley & His Comets compare themselves with?

        a. a child in a candy store

        b. a fish out of water

        c. a one-eyed cat

****

3. In *Tears on My Pillow,* what wouldn't Little Anthony & the Imperials hesitate doing?

        a. marrying you

        b. taking you back

        c. turning a page in their life

****

4. In *I Wonder Why,* what is it that Dion & the Belmonts wonder ?

        a. why you don't notice them

        b. why they love you like they do

        c. why an angel like you came into their world

5. According to Johnny Mathis, what can *A Certain Smile* do?

       a. make the day a bright bouquet

       b. make the clouds drift away

       c. haunt your heart

****

6. How does Ricky Nelson describe the eyes of the girl who tricked him into being a *Poor Little Fool*?

       a. as soft and bewitching

       b. as eyes without a soul

       c. as carefree devil eyes

****

7. Although they were a *Big Man,* what do the Four Preps now say?

       a. boy, you ought to see them now

       b. man, it only gets better from here

       c. wow, they're growing every day

****

8. In *Footsteps,* where do Frankie Lymon & the Teenagers say they hang out?

    a. outside your bedroom window

    b. on the corner where they used to meet you

    c. at the local malt shop with the juke box blasting

9. In *Oh Boy!* what do the Crickets say makes everything right?

    a. your sweet kiss

    b. a little bit of lovin'

    c. when you tell them you'll always stay

****

10. What do the Elegants ask the *Little Star*?

    a. where are you?

    b. why do you shine so bright?

    c. where's your older sister?

****

11. In *Rock & Roll is Here to Stay,* what do Danny & the Juniors tell people who don't like rock 'n roll?

    a. you're way behind the times

    b. you're square, daddy-o

    c. think of what you've been missing

****

12. How do the Four Lads reply when they ask *Who Needs You?*

    a. that they do

    b. that you do

    c. that all the world does

13. According to Ricky Nelson in *It's Late,* what time should they have left home to have plenty of time?

       a. 7:00

       b. 8:45

       c. noon

****

14. What is it that the Platters say *You'll Never Never Know*?

     a. the torch they bear

     b. how sorry they are

     c. the rivers they have to cross for you

****

15. In *Along Came Jones,* how do the Coasters describe Jones?

      a. as mean and dirty

      b. as tall, thin & slow-walkin'

      c. as slick and quick on the draw

****

16. According to Bobby Darin, who disappeared just around the time *Mack the Knife* got back in town?

       a. his wife's lover

       b. Jackie Paper

       c. Louie Miller

HARDER QUESTIONS (17-20): 2 points each
(4 points if you can answer the question without the three choices !)

17. In *Don't Let Go,* what is the one thing that Roy Hamilton won't tolerate?

   a. your lips kissing some other man

   b. you partying all night and coming home late

   c. you spending all of his hard-earned cash

****

18. After Russ Hamilton buys you a *Rainbow,* what will he buy next?

        a. a ring

        b. the moon

        c. the world

****

19. In *Don't You Just Know It,* Huey Smith & the Clowns ask if you can _____.

        a. go slowly

        b. dance with them

        c. give them a chance

****

20. Because of their *Lonely Nights,* what do the Hearts want you to do?

        a. call

        b. come home

        c. make love to them

Quiz 3

1. **c.** a frog
2. **c.** a one-eyed cat
3. **b.** taking you back
4. **b.** why they love you like they do
5. **c.** haunt your heart
6. **c.** as carefree devil eyes
7. **a.** boy, you ought to see them now
8. **b.** on the corner where they used to meet you
9. **b.** a little bit of lovin'
10. **a.** where are you?
11. **c.** think of what you've been missing
12. **a.** that they do
13. **b.** 8:45
14. **a.** the torch they bear
15. **b.** as tall, thin & slow-walkin'
16. **c.** Louie Miller

****

Questions 17-20: **HARDER QUESTIONS**

17. **a.** your lips kissing some other man
18. **b.** the moon
19. **a.** go slowly
20. **b.** come home

Quiz 4

1. Although he says he's got everything one could ever think of, what is it that Paul Anka, the *Lonely Boy*, really wants?

    a. a place of his very own
    b. someone to love
    c. peace of mind

****

2. From what state is Chuck Berry's *Johnny B. Goode*?

    a. Louisiana
    b. Mississippi
    c. Tennessee

****

3. In *Blue Suede Shoes,* what does Carl Perkins say it's OK to step on?

    a. his face
    b. his feet
    c. the hot asphalt

****

4. When does Bobby Rydell say is *Kissin' Time*?

    a. all the time
    b. summertime
    c. when the lights go down

5. In *Good Luck Charm*, what would Elvis Presley do if he had a lucky penny?

      a. he'd sell it at the coin show

      b. he'd give it to you

      c. he'd toss it across the bay

****

6. What time is it when the Everly Brothers are asking their date to *Wake Up Little Susie*?

      a. 4:00 a.m.

      b. midnight

      c. noon

****

7. How do the Penguins describe themselves in their relationship with their *Earth Angel*?

      a. they're halfway to paradise

      b. they're your puppet

      c. they're a fool in love with you

****

8. In *To Know Him is To Love Him*, what do the Teddy Bears' friends say will happen?

a. he'll leave them one day alone and broken-hearted

b. their love will continue to grow throughout eternity

c. there will come a day when they'll walk alongside of him

9. What does Chuck Berry's *Sweet Little Sixteen* wear to the dance?

    a. a tight dress and high-heeled shoes

    b. tennis shoes with pink shoe laces

    c. a tear-away blouse and polka-dot undies

****

10. When Wilbert Harrison is standing on the corner in *Kansas City,* what will he be carrying with him?

    a. your love

    b. a bottle of wine

    c. his American Express card

****

11. For Buddy Holly, *Everyday* is going faster than _____.

    a. the day before

    b. a bat out of hell

    c. a roller coaster

****

12. What is Marty Robbins all dressed up in a *White Sport Coat* for?

    a. a car-race

    b. a dance

    c. a rodeo

13. In *Put Your Head on My Shoulder,* what do some people tell Paul Anka that love really is?

    a. a duel to the finish

    b. the key to happiness

    c. a game you can't win

****

14. According to Johnny Burnette in *You're Sixteen,* when did they both fall in love?

    a. on the day they were born

    b. on the night they met

    c. when she turned sixteen

****

15. In *Don't Be Cruel,* Elvis Presley says that if you can't come around, what else can you do?

    a. telephone

    b. write to him

    c. watch him on television

****

16. In *Why Do Fools Fall in Love,* who do Frankie Lymon & the Teenagers say await the break of day?

    a. birds

    b. fools

    c. lovers

17. What does Buddy Holly say will happen *Early in the Morning* one of these days?

      a. you're gonna miss him

      b. he'll be comin' for your love

      c. there will be a new sun a-risin'

****

18. Because *You Cheated,* what is all that the Shields can do?

      a. find someone new

      b. keep on loving you

      c. learn to live with all your lies

****

19. What do Lewis Lymon & the Teenchords say that other people accuse them of being *Too Young* to do?

      a. be in love

      b. get married

      c. go out on the town

****

20. Until around what time does Fats Domino say *I'm Ready* to rock & roll with you?

      a. the midnight hour

      b. three o'clock in the morning

      c. the time the sun comes up

1. **b**. someone to love
2. **a**. Louisiana
3. **a**. his face
4. **b**. summertime
5. **c**. he'd toss it across the bay
6. **a**. 4:00 a.m.
7. **c**. they're a fool in love with you
8. **c**. there will come a day when they'll walk alongside of him
9. **a**. a tight dress and high-heeled shoes
10. **b**. a bottle of wine
11. **c**. a roller coaster
12. **b**. a dance
13. **c**. a game you can't win
14. **b**. on the night they met
15. **a**. telephone
16. **c**. lovers

****

Questions 17-20: **HARDER QUESTIONS**

17. **a**. you're gonna miss him
18. **b**. keep on loving you
19. **a**. be in love
20. **b**. three o'clock in the morning

Quiz 5

1. According to Frankie Avalon, *A Boy Without A Girl* is like _____.

       a. a day without sunshine

       b. a song without a tune

       c. a fish without a bicycle

****

2. Since what event occurred in *Donna* has Ritchie Valens never been the same?

  a. since his girlfriend left him

  b. since his girlfriend won his heart

  c. since his girl moved out of the neighborhood

****

3. Although the Del-Vikings want to tell you how much they love you and to ask if you'll *Come Go With Me,* why can't they succeed in their mission?

  a. because you never give them a chance

  b. because you belong to someone else

  c. because they don't know the right words to say

****

4. Who did Bobby Day's *Rockin' Robin* out-bop?

       a. the eagles

       b. the ravens

       c. the buzzards

5. In *Hushabye,* what do the Mystics call to the guardian angels up above to do?

    a. give them an angel to love

    b. quit bothering them with thoughts of love

    c. take care of the one they love

****

6. What does Fats Domino have to do on *Blue Monday*?

    a. get out of bed and clear his head

    b. look forward to another week

    c. work and slave all day

****

7. Because the *Image of a Girl* was on their mind and they couldn't sleep, what did the Safaris hear while lying on their bed?

    a. the milkman

    b. the clock

    c. her voice

****

8. According to the Kingston Trio, how is *Tom Dooley* scheduled to die?

    a. strapped to an electric chair

    b. of old age

    c. by hanging

9. According to Little Richard, who can't *Good Golly Miss Molly* hear calling while she's rockin' and rollin'?

        a. her mama

        b. her papa

        c. her neighbors

****

10. According to Elvis Presley in *Hound Dog,* what lie has he heard from others regarding his female acquaintance?

        a. that she was high-classed

        b. the she loved him

        c. that she was still a virgin

****

11. What do the Everly Brothers say that Johnny, a *Bird Dog,* made the teacher let him do?

        a. kiss her

        b. sit next to their baby

        c. lick her face

****

12. Because Eddie Cochran can't find a cure for the *Summertime Blues,* what organization does he want to present his problem before?

        a. the Rock & Roll Hall of Fame

        b. the Boy Scouts of America

        c. the United Nations

13. When do Dion & the Belmonts ask the stars above why he must be *A Teenager in Love*?

    a. every waking moment

    b. each night

    c. whenever he sees a girl walk by

****

14. Because she had *Kisses Sweeter Than Wine,* how many children did Jimmie Rodgers eventually have?

    a. four

    b. eight

    c. twelve

****

15. Where did Ray Peterson leave *Corinna, Corinna*?

    a. at the wedding chapel

    b. across the sea

    c. on the beach

****

16. How does Bobby Helms know that you are *My Special Angel*?

    a. because heaven is in your eyes

    b. because no one else in the world will do

    c. because you appear in his every dream

17. In *It's Just a Matter of Time,* what does Brook Benton caution you about your search for fortune and fame?

    a. that one man's gold is another's garbage

    b. that dreams don't always come true

    c. that what goes up must come down

****

18. When do Travis & Bob say to *Tell Him No* ?

    a. when he calls you on the telephone

    b. when he asks for a date

    c. when he wants to bring his friends along

****

19. What two people are coming to join Hank Ballard & the Midnighters for *Finger Poppin' Time* ?

    a. Steve and Candy

    b. Sue and Bobby

    c. Ike and Tina

****

20. As a *Real Wild Child,* what does Ivan say he's going to do?

    a. break loose

    b. go crazy on the dance floor

    c. go out with every girl in town

answers
Quiz 5

1. **b**. a song without a tune
2. **a**. since his girlfriend left him
3. **a**. because you never give them a chance
4. **c**. the buzzards
5. **c**. take care of the one they love
6. **c**. work and slave all day
7. **b**. the clock
8. **c**. by hanging
9. **a**. her mama
10. **a**. that she was high-classed
11. **b**. sit next to their baby
12. **c**. the United Nations
13. **b**. each night
14. **a**. four
15. **b**. across the sea
16. **a**. because heaven is in your eyes

****

Questions 17-20: **HARDER QUESTIONS**

17. **c**. that what goes up must come down
18. **b**. when he asks for a date
19. **b**. Sue and Bobby
20. **a**. break loose

Quiz 6

1. Chuck Willis asks *What Am I Living For* if not

_____.
        a. to sing
        b. for you
        c. to be free

****

2. Who was Johnny Horton fighting against in
The Battle of New Orleans ?
        a. Martians
        b. the British
        c. the Yankees

****

3. According to the Platters in *Smoke Gets in Your Eyes*, people say that someday you'll find all who love are _____.
        a. weird
        b. blessed
        c. blind

****

4. Although Guy Mitchell has *Heartaches By the Number,* what does he say will happen the day he stops counting?
        a. his world will end
        b. a new life will begin
        c. he'll be ready for algebra

5. Elvis Presley says in *Are You Lonesome Tonight?* that if life were a play, what would commemorate Act I for him?

  a. when you both fell in love
  b. when you were born
  c. when you both met

****

6. According to Johnny Preston, what was the name of the lovely Indian maid who loved *Running Bear*?

  a. Little White Dove
  b. Walking Tree
  c. Pretty Gypsy Eyes

****

7. Because the Poni-Tails were *Born Too Late,* how do you seem to look upon them?

  a. as a kid that you won't date
  b. as her big brother
  c. as a girl whose love will soon fade

****

8. How many hours a day does Jimmy Jones work as the *Handy Man*?

  a. eight to ten
  b. fourteen
  c. twenty-four

9. According to Danny & the Juniors, who can get their kicks *At The Hop*?

        a. cats and chicks

        b. old folks and young folks

        c. anyone who wants to

****

10. Who does the Hollywood Argyles' *Alley-Oop* have as a chauffeur?

        a. his woman

        b. a dinosaur

        c. a bear-cat

****

11. According to Dinah Washington in *What a Difference a Day Makes,* what is the reason for this difference?

        a. you are

        b. her new attitude

        c. the change of seasons

****

12. What does the household say to the Silhouettes after they return unsuccessfully from their attempts to *Get a Job*?

    a. tomorrow's another day when good luck will come their way

    b. that they're lying about looking for a job

    c. that they really don't need a job that bad

13. Why wouldn't the *Purple People Eater* eat Sheb Wooley?

    a. because they were friends eternally

    b. because he was too tough

    c. because he wasn't purple

****

14. When the girl with the *Itsy Bitsy Teenie Weenie Yellow Polka-Dot Bikini* finally got the nerve to go towards the water, what does Brian Hyland say she was wearing around her?

    a. a blanket

    b. a towel

    c. a barrel

****

15. Buddy Knox says that if you'll be his *Party Doll,* what will he do in return?

    a. pay you handsomely

    b. be your puppet

    c. make love to you

****

16. According to Paul Anka, what have people said about him and *Diana*?

    a. she's so shy and he's so bold

    b. he's so young and she's so old

    c. he's so hot and she's so cold

17. In Elvis Presley's *Jailhouse Rock*, what did Number 47 say to Number 3?

   a. if you can't find a partner, use a wooden chair

   b. I'll see you in the showers

   c. you're the cutest little jailbird

****

18. According to Harry Belafonte in *Mama, Look at Bubu,* what do the children wonder about their father?

   a. why he's so ugly

   b. why he never comes around

   c. why he always has other women with him

****

19. In what chapter of *The Book of Love* do the Monotones say you discover the meaning of romance?

   a. Chapter One

   b. Chapter Three

   c. Chapter Four

****

20. According to Wink Martindale, what did the *Deck of Cards* remind the soldier of?

   a. his loneliness

   b. his girlfriend back home

   c. the Bible

Quiz 6

1. **b**. for you
2. **b**. the British
3. **c**. blind
4. **a**. his world will end
5. **c**. when you both met
6. **a**. Little White Dove
7. **a**. as a kid that you won't date
8. **c**. twenty-four
9. **a**. cats and chicks
10. **b**. a dinosaur
11. **a**. you are
12. **b**. that they're lying about looking for a job
13. **b**. because he was too tough
14. **a**. a blanket
15. **c**. make love to you
16. **b**. he's so young and she's so old

****

Questions 17-20: **HARDER QUESTIONS**

17. **c**. you're the cutest little jailbird
18. **a**. why he's so ugly
19. **b**. Chapter Three
20. **c**. the Bible

Quiz 7

1. In *Bye Bye Love,* why is it that the Everly Brothers are suddenly so free?

    a. love is here and they're in love to stay

    b. school is out and party-time is here

    c. their baby is through with them

****

2. According to Ricky Nelson, what is the only price you have to pay when you're in *Lonesome Town* ?

    a. a heart full of tears

    b. your happiness

    c. all your dreams

****

3. Who is the person the Browns are singing about in *The Three Bells* ?

    a. Jimmy Brown

    b. Ricky Shore

    c. Joey Drell

****

4. In *Seven Little Girls Sitting in the Back Seat,* what does Paul Evans wish?

a. that he could be like Fred

b. that they'd stop talking so much

c. that he could decide which girl he loves the most

5. According to Debbie Reynolds, what is so special now in the life of *Tammy*?

     a. she's pregnant
     b. she's sixteen
     c. she's in love

****

6. According to Pat Boone in *Love Letters in the Sand,* although you made a vow you would forever be true, what does he say about that vow now?

    a. it has become a reality
    b. you've made that vow with every boy in town
    c. it meant nothing to you

****

7. In *(Let Me Be Your) Teddy Bear,* why doesn't Elvis want to be a tiger?

    a. because they aren't the kind you love enough
    b. because they eat too much
    c. because they play too rough

****

8. In *A Lover's Question,* what specifically does Clyde McPhatter want to know ?

    a. why do fools fall in love ?
    b. does she loves him with all her heart ?
    c. does she mean "yes" when she says "no" ?

9. In *Beep Beep,* what model car is trying to pass the Playmates' Cadillac?

       a. a Rabbit

       b. a Rambler

       c. a Pinto

****

10. What do Little Caesar & the Romans say *Those Oldies But Goodies* are a symbol of?

  a. the music they'll always play in their heart

  b. the love they had for you

  c. the past that can never return

****

11. The Fleetwoods want you to *Come Softly to Me* from where?

      a. from within their dreams

      b. from Wonderland

      c. from up above

****

12. Besides saying *I Want to Walk You Home,* what else does Fats Domino ask if he can do?

      a. hold your hand

      b. see you tomorrow

      c. call you up

13. In *All Shook Up*, Elvis Presley's hands are

_____.

    a. shaky

    b. growing weak

    c. needing to hold you

****

14. What would Connie Francis like to do to *Stupid Cupid*?

    a. clip his wings

    b. turn his heart inside out

    c. set him straight

****

15. In *Oh! Carol,* what does Neil Sedaka call himself for letting her treat him cruel?

    a. Mister Cool

    b. a fool

    c. a guy who knows the rules

****

16. What does Freddy Cannon say you'll find *Way Down Yonder in New Orleans*?

    a. a Garden of Eden

    b. a teenage paradise

    c. a rock & roll heaven

17. In *I've Had It,* what do the Bell Notes say happens when you tell them that they should phone?

    a. they do, but your line is always busy

    b. they do, but there's nobody home

    c. you always make them feel so all alone

****

18. What does Jimmie Rodgers say is on the way to *Bimbombey*?

    a. a path of roses

    b. a house on a hill

    c. dreams and schemes and come what may

****

19. In *Happy-Go-Lucky Me,* how does Paul Evans describe his life?

    a. it's a pleasant waste of time

    b. it's just a walk in the park

    c. it's as sweet as honey

****

20. According to Mark Dinning, what did the *Teen Angel* return to the stalled automobile on the railroad tracks to retrieve?

    a. her yearbook

    b. his high school ring

    c. the car keys

Quiz 7

1. **c**. their baby is through with them
2. **a**. a heart full of tears
3. **a**. Jimmy Brown
4. **a**. that he could be like Fred
5. **c**. she's in love
6. **c**. it meant nothing to you
7. **c**. because they play too rough
8. **b**. does she loves him with all her heart?
9. **b**. a Rambler
10. **b**. the love they had for you
11. **c**. from up above
12. **a**. hold your hand
13. **a**. shaky
14. **a**. clip his wings
15. **b**. a fool
16. **a**. a Garden of Eden

****

Questions 17-20: HARDER QUESTIONS

17. **b**. they do, but there's nobody home
18. **b**. a house on a hill
19. **c**. it's as sweet as honey
20. **b**. his high school ring

Quiz 8

1. In *Devil or Angel,* what can't Bobby Vee decide?
    a. which one to go out with
    b. which one she is
    c. which one he should behave like

****

2. What does Brook Benton says he does in *So Many Ways* ?
    a. he tries to please you
    b. he tries to get you to notice him
    c. he loves you so

****

3. What do Gladys Knight & the Pips say is in *Every Beat of My Heart* ?
    a. a beat for you
    b. a burning passion
    c. a prayer for your love

****

4. Even though it is crowded, what is there still room for in Elvis Presley's *Heartbreak Hotel* ?
    a. poets and dreamers
    b. lonely musicians
    c. broken-hearted lovers

5. In *My Heart Is An Open Book,* what does some jealous so-and-so want Carl Dobkins, Jr. and you to do?

    a. part

    b. apologize

    c. leave him alone

****

6. According to Stonewall Jackson, who first met his *Waterloo*?

    a. Adam

    b. Napoleon

    c. Julius Caesar

****

7. With whom does Lloyd Price's *Stagger Lee* get in a quarrel?

    a. Slim

    b. his wife

    c. Billy

****

8. What does Jack Scott say *My True Love* really is?

    a. an angel sent from above

    b. a girl he has yet to meet

    c. a dream-lover

9. What does Gary U.S. Bonds say that every Southern belle is down in *New Orleans* ?

      a. a sight to behold

      b. a Mississippi queen

      c. a devil in disguise

****

10. According to Jimmie Rodgers in *Honeycomb*, after the Lord made a bird, what little word did He then look all around for?

      a. tweet

      b. love

      c. the

****

11. According to Bobby Darin, until he finds his *Dream Lover* what is all that he can do?

      a. keep calling and searching

      b. go to sleep and dream again

      c. keep wishing and hoping

****

12. With whom did Marty Robbins fall in love in *El Paso* ?

      a. a bar-room queen

      b. the bartender's wife

      c. a Mexican girl

13. What does Tommy Edwards ask *Please Mr. Sun* to tell his girlfriend?

       a. not to take his sunshine away

       b. just how he feels

       c. that it's raining in his heart

****

14. In *16 Candles*, the Crests describe you as their _____.

       a. dream come true

       b. midnight fantasy

       c. teenage queen

****

15. Although *It's Not for Me to Say*, what does Johnny Mathis surmise and hope might grow with each passing day?

       a. his young friend

       b. the glow of love

       c. the size of his estate

****

16. In *Let's Go, Let's Go, Let's Go,* what do Hank Ballard & the Midnighters say is taking place across town?

       a. a house party

       b. the high school dance

       c. a whole lotta trouble

HARDER QUESTIONS (17-20): 2 points each
(4 points if you can answer the question without the three choices !)

17. What two things did Chuck Berry miss until he was *Back in the U.S.A.* ?
- **a.** skyscrapers and freeways
- **b.** sunshine and girls
- **c.** taxi cabs and all-night clubs

****

18. When does Marv Johnson say that you should *Come to Me* ?
- **a.** whenever he needs you
- **b.** twenty-four hours a day
- **c.** whenever you feel that the time is right

****

19. What do the Little Dippers want you to do *Forever* ?
- **a.** keep smiling, knowing you can always count on them
- **b.** whisper sweetly that you love them
- **c.** stay by their side

****

20. What do the Tune Weavers tell the *Little Boy* not to do?
- **a.** worry about the future
- **b.** complain
- **c.** cry

Quiz 8

1. **b**. which one she is
2. **c**. he loves you so
3. **a**. a beat for you
4. **c**. broken-hearted lovers
5. **a**. part
6. **a**. Adam
7. **c**. Billy
8. **a**. an angel sent from above
9. **b**. a Mississippi queen
10. **b**. love
11. **b**. go to sleep and dream again
12. **c**. a Mexican girl
13. **b**. just how he feels
14. **c**. teenage queen
15. **b**. the glow of love
16. **a**. a house party

****

Questions 17-20: **HARDER QUESTIONS**

17. **a**. skyscrapers and freeways
18. **a**. whenever he needs you
19. **b**. whisper sweetly that you love them
20. **c**. cry

Quiz 9

1. According to Bobby Rydell, what does the *Wild One* have a new one of every day?

        a. a new car

        b. a new hair-style

        c. a new baby

****

2. In *Big Hunk o' Love,* Elvis Presley says he'd have everything his lucky charms can bring if you'd do what?

        a. give him your love

        b. kiss him

        c. let him come over tonight

****

3. According to Skip & Flip, who was eating *Cherry Pie*?

        a. they were

        b. Little Jack Horner

        c. a girl as cute as she could be

****

4. Sam Cooke tells us that the people on the *Chain Gang* work all day until _____.

        a. the sun goes down

        b. the clock strikes five

        c. they feel like giving up

5. In *Shimmy Shimmy Ko-Ko-Pop,* where were Little Anthony & the Imperials sitting all alone and blue?

    a. in a native hut

    b. in their car at the drive-in movie

    c. on a park bench staring at the morning dew

****

6. What does Frankie Avalon wish for *Venus* to bring him?

    a. lots of money

    b. a girl to thrill

    c. somebody new

****

7. When is it that Elvis Presley says that you say *Don't*?

    a. whenever he treats you rough

    b. when it's time for him to leave

    c. each time he holds you this way

****

8. What does Gene McDaniels say about the *Tower of Strength*?

    a. it's the power of love

    b. it's something he'll never be

    c. it's what every weightlifter wants to be

9. What is Ral Donner's relationship with the *Girl of My Best Friend*?

        a. he doesn't like her

        b. he's her big brother

        c. he's in love with her

****

10. What is it that Bobby Lewis has a *One Track Mind* to do?

        a. hold you tight

        b. make you smile

        c. become a famous rock star

****

11. What does Neil Sedaka say is through for his *Little Devil*?

        a. her silly games

        b. her roving days

        c. her childish ways

****

12. In *When Will I Be Loved*, what happens to the Everly Brothers every time they meet a new girl whom they want for themselves?

    a. they find out that she's already going steady

    b. she breaks their heart

    c. their heart skips a beat

13. In *G.I. Blues,* what is Elvis Presley going to do if he doesn't go stateside soon?

    a. blow a fuse

    b. turn gay

    c. write himself a letter

****

14. In *Fool #1,* what does Brenda Lee consider herself as?

    a. your master

    b. your biggest fan

    c. the biggest fool of all

****

15. In *Take Good Care of My Baby*, what does Bobby Vee want you to do if you should discover that you don't really love his sweetheart?

    a. kick her out into the street

    b. tell her that she should come back when she grows up

    c. send her back to him

****

16. What does Connie Francis say that *Frankie* will never see her do?

    a. beg

    b. cry

    c. leave

HARDER QUESTIONS (17-20): 2 points each
(4 points if you can answer the question without the three choices !)

17. In *Harbor Lights*, what did the Platters' heart whisper to them?

    a. that you would soon be back in their arms

    b. that happiness would return with the next high tide

    c. that some other harbor lights would steal your love from them

****

18. In *Down By the Station*, where did the Four Preps meet girl #2?

    a. by the malt shop

    b. at the drug store

    c. outside the restroom

****

19. While you're *Havin' Fun*, what do friends tell Dion that he is?

    a. a fool

    b. happy and in love

    c. Mr. Blue

****

20. According to Steve Lawrence, what are the *Footsteps* doing?

    a. walking all over him

    b. haunting his every thought

    c. walking away from him

answers
Quiz 9

1. **c.** a new baby
2. **b.** kiss him
3. **b.** Little Jack Horner
4. **a.** the sun goes down
5. **a.** in a native hut
6. **b.** a girl to thrill
7. **c.** each time he holds you this way
8. **b.** it's something he'll never be
9. **c.** he's in love with her
10. **a.** hold you tight
11. **b.** her roving days
12. **b.** she breaks their heart
13. **a.** blow a fuse
14. **c.** the biggest fool of all
15. **c.** send her back to him
16. **b.** cry

****
Questions 17-20: **HARDER QUESTIONS**

17. **c.** that some other harbor lights would steal your love from them
18. **a.** by the malt shop
19. **a.** a fool
20. **c.** walking away from him

Quiz 10

1. According to Ray Peterson in *Tell Laura I Love Her*, what was the name of Laura's boyfriend?

      a. Billy

      b. Tommy

      c. Johnny

****

2. In *Does Your Chewing Gum Lose Its Flavor*, what does Lonnie Donegan say you do when your mother says not to chew it?

      a. you tell her where she can stick it

      b. you stick it under your pillow

      c. you swallow it

****

3. What did the Crests do *Step by Step*?

      a. they walked away from you

      b. they fell in love with you

      c. they crept up on you

****

4. In *Walk On By*, where does Leroy Van Dyke tell you to wait for him?

      a. on the corner

      b. at his front door

      c. by the old sugar mill

5. What does Jackie Wilson say he can do as another *Night* comes around ?
   - **a.** wait for the telephone to ring
   - **b.** watch the late-late movie
   - **c.** dream about you

****

6. According to Jimmy Jones, if it hadn't been for *Good Timin',* where might you and he spend the rest of your lives?
   - **a.** in two worlds far apart
   - **b.** walking down Misery Street
   - **c.** waiting for a moment that would never come

****

7. In which month does Neil Sedaka call his *Calendar Girl* his little Valentine?
   - **a.** February
   - **b.** March
   - **c.** every month of the year

****

8. In *There's a Moon Out Tonight,* what do the Capris have that they never felt before?
   - **a.** a glow in their heart
   - **b.** a sense of belonging
   - **c.** a personality

9. At what age did Dion, the *Lonely Teenager,* run away from home?

> **a.** thirteen
> **b.** sixteen
> **c.** twenty-one

****

10. In *Pony Time,* Chubby Checker says to turn to your left when he says "gee" and turn to your right when he says _____.

> **a.** "yeah"
> **b.** "whoa"
> **c.** "halt"

****

11. Along with a note, what else did Pat Boone find while at *Moody River*?

> **a.** your shoes
> **b.** a glove
> **c.** your picture

****

12. If you tell the Shirelles now whether *Will You Love Me Tomorrow,* what won't they do?

> **a.** ask again
> **b.** continue going out with Freddy
> **c.** cheat on you

13. In Elvis Presley's *Can't Help Falling In Love,* who says that only fools rush in?

    a. those in love

    b. wise men

    c. people who've never been in love

****

14. In *Shop Around,* what does the mother of the Miracles advise them to keep for as long as they can?

    a. their sanity

    b. their virginity

    c. their freedom

****

15. Besides *Bread and Butter,* what else do the Newbeats like?

    a. toast and jam

    b. mashed potatoes

    c. peanut butter

****

16. What did the Shangri-Las' dad say one day to them about their *Leader of the Pack*?

    a. that it's better to be a leader than a follower

    b. that they'd better find someone new

    c. that he's got a lot of enemies

HARDER QUESTIONS (17-20): 2 points each
(4 points if you can answer the question without the three choices !)

17. To do *The Hucklebuck,* what does Chubby Checker say you should do?

    a. wiggle like a snake

    b. jerk back and forth

    c. quack just like a duck

****

18. On what street do Joey Dee & the Starliters want you to go to meet other fans of *The Peppermint Twist*?

    a. 7th Avenue

    b. South Street

    c. 45th Street

****

19. In *It's Just a Matter of Time,* what do the Elegants say you'll discover when that magic moment for you to kiss them is reached?

    a. that love is timeless

    b. that time didn't matter at all

    c. that it's always better to take one's time

****

20. In *Bless You,* how did Tony Orlando feel before you smiled and took his hand?

    a. like a lost child

    b. like a sinner

    c. kind of small

1. **b**. Tommy
2. **c**. you swallow it in spite
3. **b**. they fell in love with you
4. **a**. on the corner
5. **c**. dream about you
6. **b**. walking down Misery Street
7. **a**. February
8. **a**. a glow in their heart
9. **b**. sixteen
10. **c**. "halt"
11. **b**. a glove
12. **a**. ask again
13. **b**. wise men
14. **c**. their freedom
15. **a**. toast and jam
16. **b**. that they'd better find someone new

****

Questions 17-20: **HARDER QUESTIONS**

17. **a**. wiggle like a snake
18. **c**. 45th Street
19. **b**. that time didn't matter at all
20. **c**. kind of small

Quiz 11

1. Terry Stafford has *Suspicion* that when you tell him you want to see him tomorrow, he can't help but think that you're _____.

    a. going to secretly see him tonight

    b. meeting someone else tonight

    c. planning a surprise party for him

****

2. Who else in Little Eva's family can do the *Loco-Motion* with ease?

    a. her mother

    b. her babysitter

    c. her baby sister

****

3. What is it that keeps *Georgia On My Mind* for Ray Charles?

    a. memories of love

    b. her old loveletters

    c. an old sweet song

****

4. What does Bobby Vee say that no guy in town would do when he's *Walking With My Angel*?

    a. step in his way

    b. put him down

    c. try to steal her heart away

5. By what time is Lee Dorsey already up and
Working in the Coal Mine?

      a. well before dawn

      b. around midnight

      c. five o'clock in the morning

****

6. Who does Jimmy Soul suggest for you to pick
as your wife *If You Want to Be Happy*?

      a. a dream lover

      b. a younger girl

      c. an ugly girl

****

7. In *Happy Birthday Sweet Sixteen,* why does
Neil Sedaka smile in sweet surprise?

      a. because you've grown up right before his eyes

      b. because you're so easy to believe when you're
telling such lies

      c. because you've got a pair of tasty thighs

****

8. Although some people call Ricky Nelson
A Teenage Idol, what don't they have any way
of knowing?

      a. his deep, dark, secret past

      b. how lonesome he can be

      c. how happy he really is

9. In *Daydreams*, what is the only thing that Johnny Crawford does?

> **a.** dream of you
>
> **b.** sleep all day
>
> **c.** waste his time

****

10. In *Never on Sunday*, on what day do the Chordettes say is the best day to kiss them?

> **a.** Monday
>
> **b.** Friday
>
> **c.** Saturday

****

11. In *Anna (Go With Him)*, what does Arthur Alexander want her to give back to him?

> **a.** her love
>
> **b.** his ring
>
> **c.** his peace of mind

****

12. In *Quarter to Three*, what is the name of the swingingest band Gary U.S. Bonds is dancing to?

> **a.** the Dovells
>
> **b.** the Comets
>
> **c.** Daddy G

13. Although it is the Twister who is flying high in *Let's Twist Again,* what else does Chubby Checker ask if it might be?

   a. a flying saucer
   b. a tornado
   c. a bird

****

14. According to the Impalas, why is it that *I Ran All The Way Home*?

   a. someone stole their car
   b. to say they're sorry
   c. to prove how much they really love you

****

15. In *Return to Sender,* what is Elvis Presley saying in the letter he's trying to have delivered?

a. he's sorry
b. he wants you to quit bothering him and his family
c. he wants you to come over tonight

****

16. In *Sea of Love,* what event does Phil Phillips ask whether you can remember?

a. when you and he met
b. the first time you went to a drive-in movie together
c. when the moon hid behind the clouds

HARDER QUESTIONS (17-20): 2 points each
(4 points if you can answer the question without the three choices !)

17. In *Mule Skinner Blues*, where do the Fendermen say they are from?
    - a. Alabama
    - b. Kentucky
    - c. Mule country

****

18. In *Sad Movies (Make Me Cry)*, why did Sue Thompson go to the movies alone?
    - a. because her boyfriend told her he had to work
    - b. because she didn't want to let anyone else see her cry
    - c. because her friends let her down

****

19. According to Paul Anka, what was the reason that he took a little trip to *My Home Town*?
    - a. just to look around
    - b. to listen to all the sights and sounds
    - c. to reminisce about his old stomping ground

****

20. In *I'm a Fool For Loving You*, what does Bobby Edwards call himself?
    - a. a dumbhead
    - b. your second choice
    - c. just a fool who'll never learn

Quiz 11

1. **b.** meeting someone else tonight
2. **c.** her baby sister
3. **c.** an old sweet song
4. **b.** put him down
5. **c.** five o'clock in the morning
6. **c.** an ugly girl
7. **a.** because you've grown up right before his eyes
8. **b.** how lonesome he can be
9. **a.** dream of you
10. **c.** Saturday
11. **b.** his ring
12. **c.** Daddy G
13. **c.** a bird
14. **b.** to say they're sorry
15. **a.** he's sorry
16. **a.** when you and he met

****

Questions 17-20: **HARDER QUESTIONS**

17. **b.** Kentucky
18. **a.** because her boyfriend told her he had to work
19. **a.** just to look around
20. **b.** your second choice

Quiz 12

1. Why did the Everly Brothers go to the chaplain to send for their *Ebony Eyes*?
    a. because it was too late to mail her a letter
    b. because they knew their time on earth was running short
    c. because their weekend pass didn't give them enough time to get her

****

2. In *Missing You*, what is all that Ray Peterson wants to do?
    a. be kissing you
    b. go on with his life
    c. wait until you return to him

****

3. According to Dee Dee Sharp in *Mashed Potato Time*, who started the Mashed Potato?
    a. Sloppy Joe
    b. she did
    c. Chubby Checker

****

4. In *It's All in the Game*, what game is Tommy Edwards referring to?
    a. the game of love
    b. the game of life
    c. the game of heartbreak

5. What does Nat "King" Cole say you can't do to a *Ramblin' Rose*?

        a. bring it home
        b. show it off
        c. cling to it

****

6. In *(Marie's the Name of) His Latest Flame*, what does Elvis Presley say that she swore to him the day before?

    a. that she never cheated on him
    b. that she'd be his eternally
    c. that she didn't want to see him again

****

7. Why doesn't anyone want Jack to stay around in Ray Charles' *Hit the Road, Jack*?

    a. he's a wanted fugitive
    b. he's broke
    c. he never told anyone he was coming

****

8. What do the Majors hope regarding *A Wonderful Dream*?

    a. that they can have the same dream once again
    b. that it will come true
    c. that the same dream may come to you

9. Sam Cooke tells *Cupid* that he loves a girl who

_____.

       a. doesn't exist

       b. is not in love with him

       c. doesn't know he exists

****

10. In *Daddy's Home,* Shep & the Limelites want to thank you for _____.

       a. keeping the porch light on

       b. waiting patiently

       c. being a friend

****

11. Bobby Vee is treated so carelessly in *Rubber Ball* that when he's with his girlfriend, what does she call him?

       a. by some other boy's name

       b. a loser

       c. Number Six

****

12. What does Gene McDaniels say was created with *A Hundred Pounds of Clay*?

       a. love

       b. a woman

       c. a monster Gumby

13. In *Popsicles and Icicles*, the Murmaids'
boyfriend also loves baseball and

_____.
           a. hot dogs
           b. Santa Claus
           c. fancy clothes

****

14. Although Linda Scott says *I've Told Every
Little Star,* who is it that she hasn't told?
           a. her guardian angel
           b. anyone else
           c. you

****

15. According to the Tokens, where is it that *The
Lion Sleeps Tonight*?
           a. in the county zoo
           b. near a peaceful village
           c. in his favorite den

****

16. In *Wolverton Mountain,* what does Claude
King say about the daughter of Clifton
Clowers?
           a. he wants her for his wife
           b. she's the only girl in town
           c. she rarely sees the light of day

HARDER QUESTIONS (17-20): 2 points each
(4 points if you can answer the question without the three choices !)

17. According to Jimmy Dean, how many people did *Big Bad John* save from the cave-in at the mine?

> **a.** 20
> **b.** 75
> **c.** 200

****

18. In what state does Sam Cooke say they're *Twistin' the Night Away*?

> **a.** New York
> **b.** Georgia
> **c.** in every state across the USA

****

19. In *Don't Hang Up,* what do the Orlons want to have explained to them?

> **a.** who was that chick that they saw you with?
> **b.** why did you call them so late at night?
> **c.** why don't you come over anymore?

****

20. While *Ahab, the Arab* wore a turban and had emeralds and rubies dripping off of him, what does Ray Stevens say he had by his side?

> **a.** his trusty llama
> **b.** a scimitar
> **c.** three girls from the harem

1. **c**. because their weekend pass didn't give them enough time to get her

2. **a**. be kissing you

3. **a**. Sloppy Joe

4. **a**. the game of love

5. **c**. cling to it

6. **b**. that she'd be his eternally

7. **b**. he's broke

8. **b**. that it will come true

9. **c**. doesn't know he exists

10. **b**. waiting patiently

11. **a**. by some other boy's name

12. **b**. a woman

13. **c**. fancy clothes

14. **c**. you

15. **b**. near a peaceful village

16. **a**. he wants her for his wife

****

Questions 17-20: **HARDER QUESTIONS**

17. **a**. 20

18. **a**. New York

19. **a**. who was that chick that they saw you with?

20. **b**. a scimitar

Quiz 13

1. Why does Bobby Rydell say *I'll Never Dance Again* ?

a. because his feet won't let him since you went away

b. because your love has turned all his dreams into ashes

c. because someone else is holding you the way he did then

****

2. In *Johnny Get Angry,* what does Joanie Sommers want Johnny to do?

    a. show her that he really cares for her

    b. slap her silly

    c. stop going out with other girls

****

3. What do Dick & DeeDee say happens when you're *Young and In Love* ?

    a. there's nothing in the world you can't do

    b. the whole world seems to know

    c. everybody puts you down

****

4. In *What's A-Matter Baby,* what is it that Timi Yuro has found out about you?

    a. that you've been crying

    b. that you're getting married to someone else

    c. that you're not who you said you were

5. What name does Dion, *The Wanderer,* have tattooed on his chest?

    a. Dion

    b. Rosie

    c. Ruby

****

6. In *Lover Please,* what does Clyde McPhatter ask her not to do?

    a. share his love with someone new

    b. make him beg and plead

    c. leave him in misery

****

7. Although Jay & the Americans thought their romance was over and done, why was it that *She Cried*?

    a. they were tears of happiness

    b. she thought it had just begun

    c. because girls are made that way

****

8. Once Ricky Nelson said *Hello, Mary Lou,* he knew he'd said goodbye to what?

    a. the blues

    b. his freedom

    c. his heart

9. What does Gene Pitney say about *The Man Who Shot Liberty Valance*?

        a. he was a fool

        b. he was the bravest man of all

        c. he was a dead man walking

****

10. Along with the Zombies, who else appeared at Bobby "Boris" Pickett's *Monster Mash*?

        a. Frankenstein

        b. Godzilla

        c. Dracula

****

11. Why is it that Ray Charles wants you to *Unchain My Heart*?

        a. because he's found someone new

        b. because you don't care about him

        c. because love has made a prisoner of him

****

12. In *Little Sister,* what does Elvis Presley notice every time he sees her big sister?

        a. that she's got somebody new

        b. that she's getting bigger all the time

        c. that you're always around

13. What did *Her Royal Majesty* do for James Darren?

        a. she made him the king of her heart

        b. she gave him hope and inspiration

        c. she made a fool out of him

****

14. In *Cryin' in the Rain,* why do the Everly Brothers want to wait for cloudy skies?

    a. so you won't know the rain from the tears in their eyes

    b. so you won't know the truth from all their alibis

    c. so you won't see their pain when they tell you those lies

****

15. According to Dickey Lee, where did *Patches* live?

        a. down by the river

        b. by the railroad tracks

        c. in the back of a clothing store

****

16. What is it that the Marvelettes know about the *Playboy*?

    a. that he's had many lovers before

    b. that he'll bring you up just to put you down

    c. that he's a liar and a cheater and a hard–drinking guy

17. In *Boys*, what have the Shirelles been told happens when a boy kisses a girl?

      a. he takes a trip around the world

      b. he's in love to stay

      c. a star falls from the sky

****

18. Because he was so *Proud,* what else is Johnny Crawford now?

      a. in love

      b. lonely

      c. a winner

****

19. Because *Life's Too Short,* the Lafayettes want you to marry them before _____.

      a. it's too late

      b. they move away

      c. their hair turns grey

****

20. Although the Cascades say *There's a Reason* that they must cry, what do they add?

      a. that it's all because you told them a lie

      b. that you'll bring joy to another guy

      c. that they'd like to know why

Quiz 13

1. **c.** because someone else is holding you
   the way he did then
2. **a.** show her that he really cares for her
3. **b.** the whole world seems to know
4. **a.** that you've been crying
5. **b.** Rosie
6. **c.** leave him in misery
7. **b.** she thought it had just begun
8. **c.** his heart
9 **b.** he was the bravest man of all
10. **c.** Dracula
11. **b.** because you don't care about him
12. **a.** that she's got somebody new
13. **c.** she made a fool out of him
14. **a.** so you won't know the rain from the tears
   in their eyes
15. **a.** down by the river
16. **a.** that he's had many lovers before

****

Questions 17-20: **HARDER QUESTIONS**

17. **a.** he takes a trip around the world
18. **b.** lonely
19. **c.** their hair turns grey
20. **c.** that they'd like to know why

Quiz 14

1. In *Next Door to an Angel*, where did Neil Sedaka see his now-attractive neighbor walking?

   > a. along the shore
   > b. down Main Street
   > c. outside her house

****

2. When is it that Paul Petersen says *She Can't Find Her Keys* ?

   > a. during her school recess
   > b. when he takes her home at night
   > c. whenever he tries to unlock her love

****

3. When Lesley Gore says *You Don't Own Me*, she also makes it clear to her boyfriend that she's not one of his many _____.

   > a. trophies
   > b. Barbie dolls
   > c. toys

****

4. The Lettermen say that *When I Fall in Love*, how long will it last?

   > a. forever
   > b. until the twelfth of never
   > c. until one and one is three

5. In Paul & Paula's *Hey Paula,* what is it that Paul can't wait to have end?

      a. their romance

      b. summer vacation

      c. school

****

6. What is the main reason that Jimmy Gilmer & the Fireballs want to go back to the *Sugar Shack* ?

    a. there's a cute girl working there

    b. they serve the finest Espresso coffee there

    c. they want to tear the place down

****

7. In *Runaway,* what does Del Shannon ponder as he walks along?

    a. why he ever tried to protect her from the rest of the world

    b. the things they'd done together when they were young

    c. how he is going to be able to escape the gallows

****

8. What night of the week do the kids in Bristol dance to the Dovells' *Bristol Stomp* ?

      a. Friday

      b. Saturday

      c. every night

9. Although the Coasters say *Poison Ivy* is pretty as a daisy, they also caution you that she's
_____.

        a. lazy

        b. crazy

        c. nasty

****

10. When Brenda Lee says *I'm Sorry,* she asks you to _____.

        a. not take it so personally

        b. accept her apologies

        c. look for someone new

****

11. In *Everybody's Somebody's Fool,* Connie Francis knows that, even though she'll be hurt by her boyfriend whenever she sees him, what else does she concede?

  a. that one day he'll become someone else's fool

  b. that love will eventually bring them back together

  c. that she'll come running back for more

****

12. What do people tell Little Anthony & the Imperials, even though it *Hurts So Bad* ?

  a. because she's in love, don't stand in her way

  b. keep chasing after her, no matter how long it takes

  c. don't be afraid to get a medical checkup

13. In *The Name Game*, Shirley Ellis tells us that she can make a rhyme _____.

    a. out of anybody's name

    b. from any word in the dictionary

    c. if you'll give her enough time

****

14. In *My Boyfriend's Back*, what will the Angels' boyfriend restore?

    a. a lasting love

    b. their peace of mind

    c. their reputation

****

15. What do the Ad Libs' *Boy From New York City* have that is the finest in town?

    a. a penthouse

    b. a Lamborghini

    c. the coolest friends

****

16. According to the Shirelles in *Baby It's You*, what do they spend their nights doing?

    a. contemplating the morning to come

    b. crying over you

    c. dreaming about you

HARDER QUESTIONS (17-20): **2 points each**
(4 points if you can answer the question without the three choices !)

17. In *Zoom Zoom Zoom*, what do the Dreamlovers want the world to know?

    a. that they're in a hurry to meet you

    b. that you're too fast for them

    c. that they love you so

****

18. In *Nothing Can Change This Love*, what would Sam Cooke do if he were to go a million miles away?

    a. he'd write you a letter every day

    b. he'd phone to tell you that everything's okay

    c. he'd make his new home a place you could stay

****

19. In *Jimmy Mack*, about how many times a day does another boy keep calling Martha & the Vandellas?

    a. once or twice

    b. three

    c. about a hundred

****

20. What does Walter Brennan say that *Old Rivers* spent his whole life doing?

    a. nothing

    b. looking for a home

    c. walking plowed ground

1. **b**. down Main Street
2. **b**. when he takes her home at night
3. **c**. toys
4. **a**. forever
5. **c**. school
6. **a**. there's a cute girl working there
7. **b**. the things they'd done together when they were young
8. **a**. Friday
9. **b**. crazy
10. **b**. accept her apologies
11. **c**. that she'll come running back for more
12. **a**. because she's in love, don't stand in her way
13. **a**. out of anybody's name
14. **c**. their reputation
15. **a**. a penthouse
16. **b**. crying over you

****

Questions 17-20: **HARDER QUESTIONS**

17. **c**. that they love you so
18. **a**. he'd write you a letter every day
19. **b**. three
20. **c**. walking plowed ground

Quiz 15

1. What do the Four Seasons want to do all night with *Sherry*?

       a. walk along the beach

       b. dance

       c. count the stars in the sky

****

2. What does Joe Jones say *You Talk Too Much* about?

       a. people

       b. money

       c. romance

****

3. In *Da Doo Ron Ron*, what time did the Crystals' new heart-throb pick them up for a date?

       a. at 7:00 p.m.

       b. at 10:00 p.m.

       c. at midnight

****

4. In *Crying*, when did Roy Orbison's companion say goodbye to him?

       a. last year

       b. last night

       c. just today

5. In *Please Mr. Postman,* what message are the Marvelettes hoping for?

    a. a card or letter saying that their boyfriend is returning

    b. a telegram telling them that they have won the Grand Prize

    c. a reply confirming their wedding plans

****

6. What kind of party is Lesley Gore celebrating in *It's My Party*?

    a. her parent's wedding anniversary

    b. her engagement party

    c. her birthday

****

7. What is the most obvious and unusual characteristic regarding the Cookies' *Chains*?

    a. it's a groovy new dance

    b. they're easy to get caught up in

    c. you can't see them

****

8. According to Ernie K-Doe, what would be a suitable name for his *Mother-in-Law*?

    a. the Fairy Godmother

    b. King Kong

    c. Satan

9. In *Hello Mudduh, Hello Fadduh,* what kind of party does Allan Sherman say they are about to organize for Jeffrey Hardy?

       a. a going-away party
       b. a birthday party
       c. a search-party

****

10. In *Send Me Some Lovin',* what else does Sam Cooke want you to send him?

       a. bail money
       b. your picture
       c. a one-way ticket to paradise

****

11. What are Connie Stevens' *Sixteen Reasons* celebrating?

       a. how glad she is that you turned sixteen
       b. her reasons for leaving you
       c. why she loves you

****

12. What happens when *Ruby Baby* looks at Dion?

       a. she starts giggling
       b. he gets all nervous deep inside
       c. she sets his soul aflame

13. In *Rhythm of the Rain,* where do the Cascades want it to rain so their secret love will know how they feel about her?

      a. in her heart

      b. in their eyes

      c. all over the world

****

14. In general, what don't the Skyliners have *Since I Don't Have You* ?

      a. a future

      b. anything

      c. problems

****

15. What was the word of honor that Mary Wells gave to *My Guy* ?

      a. to be faithful

      b. not to tell her dad

      c. to trust him through thick and thin

****

16. What are the Drifters doing *Under the Boardwalk* ?

      a. eating popcorn with their baby

      b. making love

      c. playing cards with the gang

HARDER QUESTIONS (17-20): 2 points each
(4 points if you can answer the question without the three choices !)

17. According to Roy Orbison in *Mean Woman Blues (I Got a Woman),* his woman is so mean that he compares her to _____.

    a. a junkyard dog

    b. himself

    c. a bitch in heat

****

18. According to the Orlons, what word describes the dancing on *South Street*?

    a. elite

    b. cool

    c. groovy

****

19. In *Cards of Love,* what game are Tico & the Triumphs playing since she's gone?

    a. deuces are wild

    b. solitaire

    c. hearts

****

20. What do the Hippies want you to take away from *Memory Lane*?

    a. the rain that falls

    b. all your promises

    c. all your love letters

Quiz 15

1. **b.** dance
2. **a.** people
3. **a.** at 7:00 p.m.
4. **b.** last night
5. **a.** a card or letter saying that their boyfriend is returning
6. **c.** her birthday
7. **c.** you can't see them
8. **c.** Satan
9. **c.** a search-party
10. **b.** your picture
11. **c.** why she loves you
12. **c.** she sets his soul aflame
13. **a.** in her heart
14. **b.** anything
15. **a.** to be faithful
16. **b.** making love

****

Questions 17-20: **HARDER QUESTIONS**

17. **b.** himself
18. **a.** elite
19. **b.** solitaire
20. **a.** the rain that falls

Quiz 16

1. In *Last Kiss*, why do J. Frank Wilson & the Cavaliers say they've got to be good?
   a. so they can see their baby when they leave this world
   b. because they've been bad for far too long
   c. because their baby promised them that she'd be true as long as they were good

****

2. In *I'm Ready For Love*, how would Martha & the Vandellas feel if they were to lose in love?
   a. defeated
   b. lonely
   c. hurt

****

3. In *Just One Look*, Doris Troy says she's going to keep on scheming until _____.
   a. she passes the test of love
   b. you finally leave her alone
   c. she makes you her own

****

4. In *Baby I Love You*, what do the Ronettes love to hear you call?
   a. the radio station
   b. the quarterback signals
   c. their name

5. The Contours ask *Do You Love Me* now that they are able to do what?

        a. read

        b. dance

        c. walk again

****

6. In *Dedicated to the One I Love,* what do the Shirelles say is just before dawn?

        a. the sound of the alarm bell

        b. the darkest hour

        c. the smell of morning dew

****

7. In *We'll Sing in the Sunshine,* what does Gale Garnett say she'll never do, because its cost is too dear?

        a. leave you

        b. love you

        c. hire a band to play after dark

****

8. When Gene Chandler, the *Duke of Earl,* holds his sweetheart, what position is she transformed into?

        a. his slave

        b. a duchess

        c. her royal majesty

9. While at *Palisades Park,* where were they when Freddy Cannon gave his girl a hug?

      a. at the top of the Ferris wheel

      b. in the tunnel of love

      c. at the ticket counter

****

10. In *Since I Fell For You,* Lenny Welch cautions that when you give love but never get love in return, then you had best _____.

      a. let love depart

      b. keep trying until love succeeds

      c. take a better look at love

****

11. In *Walk Right In,* the Rooftop Singers mention that everybody's talking about a new way of _____.

      a. smooching

      b. walking

      c. living

****

12. In *Goodbye Cruel World,* what does James Darren plan to do?

      a. jump off the highest steeple

      b. say goodbye to you

      c. join the circus

13. In *Shoop Shoop Song (It's In His Kiss)*, what does Betty Everett have to say to the idea that a warm embrace will tell you if he loves you?
> a. that's true, but it's only half the answer
> b. no, that's just his arm
> c. no, that just tells you he's still alive

****

14. Because *The Night Has a Thousand Eyes,* what does Bobby Vee say that he can tell?
> a. if you no longer care for him
> b. if you're robbing him blind
> c. if you aren't true to him

****

15. In *The End,* Earl Grant says that if you tell him you love him, what will happen to this love you share?
> a. it will suddenly end
> b. it will go on until the end of time
> c. it will not change the way he feels in the end

****

16. Where does Roy Orbison first see *Oh Pretty Woman* ?
> a. uptown
> b. down the street
> c. on the movie screen

HARDER QUESTIONS (17-20): 2 points each
(4 points if you can answer the question without the three choices !)

17. In *Baby the Rain Must Fall,* what two things does Glenn Yarbrough not love for?

    a. silver or gold

    b. fame or fortune

    c. happiness or pleasure

****

18. Because *I Sold My Heart to the Junkman,* what do the Blue-Belles say they'll never do again?

    a. fall in love

    b. take out the garbage

    c. let their eyes tell them lies

****

19. According to the Dovells, what does everyone call *Bristol Twistin' Annie* ?

    a. a pistol-whippin' girl

    b. the queen of the hop

    c. the prettiest girl they ever did see

****

20. In *My Boomerang Won't Come Back,* what did Charlie Drake discover was the one thing he forgot to do first?

    a. throw it

    b. aim it properly

    c. take it out of the box

Quiz 16

1. **a.** so they can see their baby when they leave this world
2. **c.** hurt
3. **c.** she makes you her own
4. **c.** their name
5. **b.** dance
6. **b.** the darkest hour
7. **b.** love you
8. **b.** a duchess
9. **b.** in the tunnel of love
10. **a.** let love depart
11. **b.** walking
12. **c.** join the circus
13. **b.** no, that's just his arm
14. **c.** if you aren't true to him
15. **b.** it will go on until the end of time
16. **b.** down the street

****

Questions 17-20: **HARDER QUESTIONS**

17. **a.** silver or gold
18. **a.** fall in love
19. **b.** the queen of the hop
20. **a.** throw it

Quiz 17

1. According to Brian Hyland in *Sealed With a Kiss*, what kind of summer is he going to spend?

   a. a happy and carefree one

   b. an impatient one

   c. a cold and lonely one

****

2. In *Judy's Turn to Cry*, what is the name of Lesley Gore's boyfriend?

   a. Johnny

   b. Bobby

   c. Tommy

****

3. In *Bobby's Girl*, what does Marcie Blane pray will happen one day?

   a. that she'll have him all to herself

   b. that Bobby will eventually find the girl of his dreams

   c. that Bobby will marry her

****

4. Now that *School Is Out*, what does Gary U.S. Bonds just have time to do?

   a. take his girl out on a date

   b. hand in the final exam

   c. go surfing

5. In *It Hurts to Be In Love,* because Gene Pitney is in love with somebody who considers him as a friend, what is the only way he can keep her?

    a. by chaining her to his bed
    b. by keeping it to himself
    c. by pretending that she's in love with him

****

6. If Del Shannon and his girlfriend have to *Keep Searchin',* what will they follow to guide them?

    a. the sun
    b. their dreams
    c. the yellow–brick road

****

7. Chubby Checker is going to do *The Twist* until what happens?

    a. their folks come home
    b. they get too tired to Twist anymore
    c. they tear the house down

****

8. In *Another Saturday Night,* why does Sam Cooke have spending money?

    a. he just pawned his watch
    b. he just got paid
    c. his folks gave him an advance

9. In *Johnny Angel*, how does Shelley Fabares feel when other guys call her to go out on a date with them?

    a. she'd rather concentrate on Johnny Angel

    b. she finds it hard to resist their charms

    c. she feels flattered but afraid to take the chance

****

10. What do the Shirelles ask their *Soldier Boy* to take along with him to any port or foreign shore?

    a. their picture

    b. their love

    c. proper safeguards

****

11. In *Save the Last Dance for Me*, what do the Drifters compare the music in the party with?

    a. wine

    b. happiness

    c. the fruit punch

****

12. What is Connie Francis wishing in *Where the Boys Are*?

    a. that someone is waiting for her

    b. that she'll meet her surfer boy

    c. that her friends will also be there

13. In *Blowin' in the Wind,* Peter, Paul & Mary ponder over how many ears one person must have before he can hear _____.

    a. the bombs exploding

    b. what they're saying

    c. people crying

****

14. Because men will be men, what does Jack Jones say in *Wives and Lovers* that you shouldn't do when you send your man off to work?

    a. expect him to come straight home afterwards

    b. push him out the door

    c. put your hair in curlers

****

15. What part of *Sheila* drives Tommy Roe insane?

    a. her eyes

    b. her name

    c. her lips

****

16. What happened, in *Who Put the Bomp,* when Barry Mann's girlfriend heard "bomp-a-bomp" in the music?

    a. she went quite insane

    b. she slapped him

    c. it went right into her heart

HARDER QUESTIONS (17-20): 2 points each
(4 points if you can answer the question without the three choices !)

17. In *What Time Is It,* what time are the Jive Five waiting for?

  a. six o'clock

  b. eight o'clock

  c. twelve o'clock

****

18. In *Snap Your Fingers,* what does Joe Henderson want you to give him some kind of clue about?

  a. whether or not he has a chance with you

  b. whether or not he can take you home

  c. whether he should stay or go

****

19. What does Johnny Cymbal say that *Mr. Bass Man* does to the music?

  a. he gives the music soul

  b. he sets the music thumping

  c. he makes the music go down down down

****

20. In *Baby Workout,* what does Jackie Wilson want you to do some more here on the floor?

  a. rock

  b. twist

  c. shake it up

Quiz 17

1. **c.** a cold and lonely one
2. **a.** Johnny
3. **a.** that she'll have him all to herself
4. **a.** take his girl out on a date
5. **b.** by keeping it to himself
6. **a.** the sun
7. **c.** they tear the house down
8. **b.** he just got paid
9. **a.** she'd rather concentrate on Johnny Angel
10. **b.** their love
11. **a.** wine
12. **a.** that someone is waiting for her
13. **c.** people crying
14. **c.** put your hair in curlers
15. **b.** her name
16. **c.** it went right into her heart

****

Questions 17-20: **HARDER QUESTIONS**

17. **b.** eight o'clock
18. **c.** whether he should stay or go
19. **b.** he sets the music thumping
20. **a.** rock

Quiz 18

1. With what fairy-tale character does Jimmy Clanton associate his *Venus in Blue Jeans,* adding that he adores her?
   - a. Goofy
   - b. Snow White
   - c. Cinderella

****

2. When Bruce Channel says *Hey! Baby,* what does he want to know?
   - a. if you'll be his girl
   - b. your name
   - c. how he was lucky enough to ever have met you

****

3. As long as Ben E. King knows you'll *Stand By Me,* what cataclysmic event still won't cause him to shed a tear?
   - a. if a riot should tear his town apart
   - b. if the mountains should crumble to the sea
   - c. if his whole world were to shatter

****

4. What does Marty Robbins want the *Devil Woman* to do?
   - a. leave him alone
   - b. tempt him with her charms
   - c. let him make an angel out of her

5. How do the Chiffons describe their dreamboat in *He's So Fine*?

      a. as the answer to all their prayers
      b. as a love unfulfilled
      c. as a soft-spoken guy

****

6. When Maurice Williams & the Zodiacs ask you to *Stay,* how do your folks feel according to Maurice?

      a. they're filled with rage
      b. they don't think you should
      c. they don't mind

****

7. In *Break It To Me Gently,* if you must leave, how does Brenda Lee want you to go?

      a. without saying a word
      b. as soon as possible
      c. slowly

****

8. What is Johnny Crawford going to write for *Cindy's Birthday*?

      a. a love letter
      b. a symphony
      c. a birthday card

9. When their boyfriend is with them *Uptown,* what do the Crystals say he is?

      a. a beast

      b. a king

      c. just another face in the crowd

****

10. What do the Impressions say *It's All Right* to do?

      a. get angry once in a while

      b. have a good time

      c. fall in love

****

11. In *Go Away Little Girl,* why does Steve Lawrence say that his lips and yours must never meet?

      a. because you're only thirteen

      b. because he belongs to someone else

      c. because your folks would never agree

****

12. In *Frankie and Johnny,* what does Sam Cooke say that Frankie pulled out of her pocketbook when she saw Johnny with another girl?

      a. a gun

      b. a knife

      c. a divorce decree

13. Roy Orbison says *Only the Lonely* must take a chance if they wish to find _____.

    a. happiness

    b. heaven

    c. romance

****

14. Who told the Four Seasons to give up their girlfriend and *Walk Like a Man*?

    a. their friends

    b. the camp counselor

    c. their father

****

15. In *You Beat Me to the Punch,* what is the last thing Mary Wells did, which beat you to the punch?

    a. she walked away

    b. she told your friends that you were gay

    c. she kissed you in a most unusual way

****

16. According to Eydie Gorme, *Blame It on the Bossa Nova* because it's the dance of _____.

    a. love

    b. guilty pleasures

    c. youth

17. In *Tell Me Why*, what is it that Bobby Vinton never dreamed of?

    a. romance

    b. saying goodbye

    c. going to the senior prom with you

****

18. What did his brother say when asked for a loan because Ray Charles was *Busted*?

a. that there wasn't much he could do to help out

b. that it was high time he found a job or hit the road

c. that he was going to ask him for a loan because he was also busted

****

19. Where does Claudine Clark see the *Party Lights*?

    a. next door

    b. across the street

    c. outside her bedroom window

****

20. In *From a Jack to a King*, what did Ned Miller do?

    a. he bet his life and won a wife

    b. he played an ace and won a queen

    c. he bet the house and found a spouse

1. **c**. Cinderella
2. **a**. if you'll be his girl
3. **b**. if the mountains should crumble to the sea
4. **a**. leave him alone
5. **c**. as a soft–spoken guy
6. **c**. they don't mind
7. **c**. slowly
8. **b**. a symphony
9. **b**. a king
10. **b**. have a good time
11. **b**. because he belongs to someone else
12. **a**. a gun
13. **c**. romance
14. **c**. their father
15. **a**. she walked away
16. **a**. love

****

Questions 17-20: **HARDER QUESTIONS**

17. **a**. romance
18. **c**. that he was going to ask him for a loan because he was also busted
19. **b**. across the street
20. **b**. he played an ace and won a queen

Quiz 19

1. Who does Dion's *Donna the Prima Donna* want to be like?

> **a.** the Mona Lisa
> **b.** Marilyn Monroe
> **c.** Zsa Zsa Gabor

****

2. Where is it that Elvis Presley says you should *Follow That Dream*?

> **a.** wherever that dream may lead
> **b.** straight to your lover's heart
> **c.** down the road to Rio

****

3. Where is it that Little Peggy March says *I Will Follow Him*?

> **a.** to the ends of the earth
> **b.** down the aisle of love
> **c.** wherever he may go

****

4. In *Forget Him*, Bobby Rydell wants you to drop your new boyfriend and _____.

> **a.** come home to him
> **b.** give up on love
> **c.** follow your heart

5. In *I Can't Stay Mad at You*, what does Skeeter Davis say you can be sure of?

    a. that she won't fall in love with someone new

    b. that she will always follow you

    c. that there's nothing you can't do

****

6. In *White On White*, what is Danny Williams' "little angel" doing today?

    a. moving away

    b. getting married

    c. earning her wings

****

7. The Four Seasons claim that the notion *Big Girls Don't Cry* is just _____.

    a. a fact of life

    b. an alibi

    c. what young girls say

****

8. At which port is Ricky Nelson's China girl waiting for her *Travelin' Man*?

    a. Hong Kong

    b. Shanghai

    c. Taiwan

9. When Bobby Lewis got up in the middle of the night from *Tossin' and Turnin'* to get a bite to eat, what time was the clock striking?
  a. midnight
  b. one o'clock
  c. four o'clock

****

10. Although Dee Clark wants to bring back his sweetheart in *Raindrops,* what is the problem that prevents him from being able to do so?
  a. she's no longer in this world
  b. she doesn't want to return
  c. he doesn't know where she's gone

****

11. Dobie Gray says that when you're with *The "In" Crowd,* it's easy to find _____.
  a. drugs
  b. romance
  c. kicks

****

12. What is it that Chuck Berry says the old folks say that goes to show that *You Never Can Tell*?
  a. vaya con Dios
  b. auf Wiedersehen
  c. c'est la vie

13. What is the reason Rick Nelson says now *It's Up to You*?

      a. he's ready to fall in love

      b. he's done everything he can

      c. he doesn't see any reason to go on

****

14. Who else does Bobby Vinton say will one day write that *Roses Are Red*?

      a. your daughter's boyfriend

      b. the neighborhood florist

      c. his little girl

****

15. What does Elvis Presley's *Bossa Nova Baby* say she can do with a drink in her hand?

      a. dance

      b. hail a cab

      c. make love

****

16. According to the Drifters, what won't one thin dime do for you *On Broadway*?

      a. get you a friend

      b. buy you a cup of coffee

      c. shine your shoes

HARDER QUESTIONS (17-20): 2 points each
(4 points if you can answer the question without the three choices !)

17. When is it that Chuck Jackson says *I Don't Want To Cry* ?

    a. when you turn and walk away

    b. when you tell him that it's over

    c. before you smile and walk through the door

****

18. In *Talk Back Trembling Lips,* how does Johnny Tillotson describe his love with you?

    a. as a battle royale

    b. as paradise on earth

    c. as an emotional rollercoaster

****

19. According to the Dixie Belles, what is hanging on the door *(Down at) Papa Joe's* ?

    a. a dart board

    b. a welcome sign

    c. a picture of Papa Joe

****

20. In *I Wanna Love Him So Bad,* what is the name of the new boy who has just moved into the Jelly Beans' neighborhood?

    a. Bill

    b. Jim

    c. Johnny

Quiz 19

1. **c.** Zsa Zsa Gabor

2. **a.** wherever that dream may lead

3. **c.** wherever he may go

4. **a.** come home to him

5. **a.** that she won't fall in love with someone new

6. **b.** getting married

7. **b.** an alibi

8. **a.** Hong Kong

9. **c.** four o'clock

10. **c.** he doesn't know where she's gone

11. **b.** romance

12. **c.** c'est la vie

13. **b.** he's done everything he can

14. **a.** your daughter's boyfriend

15. **a.** dance

16. **c.** shine your shoes

****

Questions 17-20: HARDER QUESTIONS

17. **c.** before you smile and walk through the door

18. **a.** as a battle royale

19. **b.** a welcome sign

20. **b.** Jim

Quiz 20

1. What is the prayer that the Duprees share with
   The Sand and the Sea ?
       a. that the world will live in peace and harmony
       b. that you'll soon be with them
       c. that they'll find their way back home

****

2. Though *He's Sure the Boy I Love*, the Crystals
   admit that he doesn't _____.
           a. drive a Cadillac
           b. really have a clue
           c. like them very much

****

3. In *Burning Bridges,* what did Jack Scott do with
   the letters he found that came from you ?
           a. he buried them
           b. he burned them
           c. he read them all aloud

****

4. What is it that Tommy Roe says *Everybody*
   has had ?
           a. the blues
           b. a dream that can't come true
           c. their fifteen minutes of fame

5. What do Martha & the Vandellas question about their *Heat Wave*?

    a. will the rain ever come down to cool their desire?

    b. is this the way love's supposed to be?

    c. does the feeling go away as time goes by?

****

6. Why do the Chiffons caution others to stay away from the *Sweet Talkin' Guy* and not give him love?

    a. because he belongs to them

    b. because tomorrow he's on his way

    c. because in nine months you'll have a sweet–talkin' baby

****

7. In *Don't Think Twice (It's Alright)*, although Peter, Paul & Mary loved a woman and gave her their heart, what did she really want?

    a. their soul

    b. their money

    c. a guarantee

****

8. In *People Get Ready,* where do the Impressions say the train is headed for?

    a. freedom

    b. heaven

    c. Jordan

9. When Lou Christie settles down in *Lightnin'*
Strikes, what does he want on his mind?

       a. all the girls he's loved before
       b. memories
       c. one woman

****

10. Because he's *Mr. Lonely,* what does Bobby
Vinton yearn to do?

       a. go back home
       b. meet someone else who cares
       c. go out and party all night long

****

11. In *Crying in the Chapel,* what does Elvis
Presley say you'll never find, even though you
may search and search?

       a. a cure for the summertime blues
       b. the girl who will always treat you fine
       c. the way on earth to gain peace of mind

****

12. In *Navy Blue,* for how long will Diane Renay
be able to see her sailor boyfriend?

       a. for an hour or two
       b. for forty-eight hours
       c. for the rest of her life

13. According to Astrud Gilberto, when *The Girl from Ipanema* walks to the sea, where are her eyes focused?

> **a.** toward the clouds
> **b.** on your eyes
> **c.** straight ahead

****

14. Why do the Four Seasons tell you to *Save It For Me*?

> **a.** because their love is true love
> **b.** because they're coming home to your arms
> **c.** because what you save today can bring happiness tomorrow

****

15. Name one thing Sam Cooke says you should *Shake* your body like?

> **a.** a rattlesnake
> **b.** a hula hoop
> **c.** a bowl of soup

****

16. In *Last Chance to Turn Around,* what is Gene Pitney planning to do now that he caught his girl cheating on him?

> **a.** have his secretary write a letter to his lawyer
> **b.** get even the best way he knows how
> **c.** get out of town

17. In *Talk to Me,* what do Sunny & the Sunglows want you to tell them?

    a. that you love them so

    b. that you'll call them every night

    c. that they're the only one for you

****

18. In *What Kind of Fool (Do You Think I Am),* what do the Tams say they won't be?

    a. your second choice

    b. your personal slave

    c. your hand-me-down

****

19. In *Harlem Shuffle,* what do Bob & Earl say you should do?

    a. wave your hands in the air

    b. scratch like a monkey

    c. strum your thumb

****

20. In *Funny (How Time Slips Away),* what does Joe Hinton remark?

a. that you get more beautiful with each passing day

b. that there's little else that he can say

c. that it seems like only yesterday

Quiz 20

1. b. that you'll soon be with them

2. a. drive a Cadillac

3. b. he burned them

4. a. the blues

5. b. is this the way love's supposed to be?

6. b. because tomorrow he's on his way

7. a. their soul

8. c. Jordan

9. c. one woman

10. a. go back home

11. c. the way on earth to gain peace of mind

12. b. for forty-eight hours

13. c. straight ahead

14. b. because they're coming home to your arms

15. c. a bowl of soup

16. c. get out of town

****

Questions 17-20: **HARDER QUESTIONS**

17. a. that you love them so

18. a. your second choice

19. b. scratch like a monkey

20. c. that it seems like only yesterday

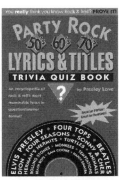
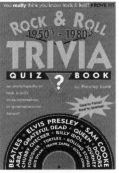
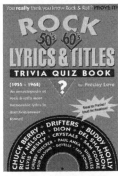
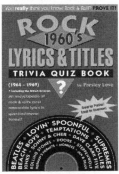
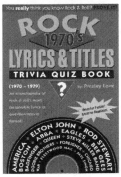
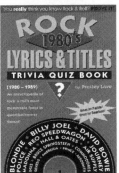

Made in the USA
Lexington, KY
13 August 2019